HOW CAN WE BELIEVE IN GOD?

CW01589922

Taletellers

HOW CAN WE BELIEVE IN GOD?

Study Guide to

WE BELIEVE IN GOD

A Report by the Doctrine Commission
of the General Synod of the Church of England

SPCK

First published in 1988
SPCK
Holy Trinity Church
Marylebone Road
London NW1 4DU

Copyright © The Taletellers 1988

All rights reserved. No part of this book may be reproduced or transmitted in any form or by any means, electronic or mechanical, including photocopying, recording, or by any information storage and retrieval system, without permission in writing from the publisher.

We Believe in God, the Report by the Doctrine Commission of the General Synod of the Church of England, is published by Church House Publishing and is © The Central Board of Finance of the Church of England 1987, by whose permission the extensive quotations in this Study Guide are used.

British Library Cataloguing in Publication Data

How can we believe in God? :Study guide
to We believe in God.
1. Church of England. Christian doctrine
God.
I. Taletellers II. Church of England,
*Doctrine Commission.*We believe in God.
23)

ISBN 0–281–04383–3

Typeset by Deltatype Ltd, Ellesmere Port
Printed in Great Britain by
The Camelot Press Ltd, Southampton

CONTENTS

FOREWORD

This Study Guide to *We Believe in God*, The Church of England Doctrine Commission's Report, is a valuable experience in theological education. As people use it, they will be fulfilling the desire of General Synod to give more strength and definition to the content of belief among members of the Church of England. It may also encourage some to work through the Report for themselves.

The writers of this Study Guide have done a marvellous job in bringing out key ideas in each section and in suggesting ways for the theologically inexperienced to begin to grasp the thought of the original Report. All of us who, as members of the Doctrine Commission, were engaged on the Report are grateful that our necessarily condensed and often technically academic work has been made accessible to a wider readership than we ourselves could ever have reached.

We Believe in God marks a significant development in our Church's teaching ministry. From one angle it is a natural successor to *Christian Believing* (1976) and *Believing in the Church* (1981). But whereas these have focused on problems for belief, and on ways in which individuals and groups believe and express their beliefs, this new report is concerned with the *content* of such belief. It takes the fundamental tenet of belief in God, and asks what that implies for people today who stand in the Christian tradition.

The Report comes at its subject from a number of different angles. It listens to what the Bible has to say. It asks what the words mean which we use about God. It thinks about God in the ways scientists think. It explores the convictions and practices of folk-religion. It faces thc demanding link between belief in God and ethical action. It enters into what people have experienced of God in prayer. In the final chapter it asks what is the inmost character of God in his personal relationship to his world.

This makes it, to my way of thinking, more widely useful than an abstract theological treatise, however profound, which argues its way steadily from A to Z of its subject. This convergent approach, from many points of the human compass, offers more people the chance of a way into the idea of God which will answer to their experience or resonate with their own heart.

It also makes it a good basis for a guide for study groups. Each member of a group will be starting from their own point of the compass, and will therefore be able to bring that journey alive to others. By the end, everyone's vision of God will, one hopes, have been enlarged and their sympathies with other believers extended.

May God bless the use of this Study Guide, and those who have so thoughtfully and skilfully laboured to produce it.

† *John Sarum*

Chairman, The Doctrine Commission

INTRODUCTION

The writings of the Doctrine Commission cannot be 'popular' in every sense of that overworked word. We hope however that We Believe in God *will be accessible to a large number of interested readers. We hope also that, where appropriate, it will be possible for the Commission's ideas to be communicated to a still wider readership. (page x)*

This Study Guide is offered as one response to this request in the Chairman's Introduction to the Report. It aims to give a map of the terrain of the Report in the hope that some will be encouraged to go to the original and grapple with it. However, the ideas in the Report are too important to be restricted to those with the time, energy and technical skill to do that. The making of doctrine, as the Report's predecessor *Believing in the Church* pointed out, belongs to the whole People of God. So this Study Guide also aims to help the 'person in the pew' to understand the issues raised by the Report and contribute to the debate. It therefore stands on its own.

The authors have tried to select some of the significant ideas in the Report and explore them through group exercises, reflections and quotation. Some of the quotations have been adapted in order to keep them reasonably short; what appear to be qualifying phrases have been left out to offer the 'bones' of the argument. All the references, however, have been given so the inquiring reader can easily check against the original. Some ideas have been omitted; the Report is a very rich mixture. Other authors would have made a different selection, but not everything can be included.

Underlying the whole exercise is, however, a more profound aim. It is that, as the result of using this Guide, Christians will be able to make their prayers more intelligent and their intelligence more prayerful. There are never going to be easy answers for Christians who want to take seriously the discoveries and movements of the modern world. It will always be a struggle, but the authors believe that the God who made the world also gave humans a mind to explore its mysteries and perplexities. The same God is also alongside them in that exploration. To paraphrase Simone Weil, 'If, in the search for truth, it appears that the path seems to turn away from Christ, it will not be long before he will be seen again, waiting further along the path.' It is that belief that changes what seems to be a human search into an exploration of prayer. For, ultimately, it is only in prayer that God is to be encountered. And it then feels that it is God who is doing the encountering.

KEY

These symbols denote the five kinds of activity in this Study Guide:

TO DO — An exercise for the group to do.

TO READ — A passage for the group to read.

TO PONDER — Material for contemplation.

TO PRAY — Material for prayer.

AT HOME — An exercise to do between meetings.

NOTES FOR LEADERS

The aim of the Study Guide is to present the range of ideas in the Doctine Commission's Report, *We Believe in God*, in such a way that people are helped to understand the issues it raises and to contribute to the debate about them. As a result, it is hoped that Christians will be able to make their prayers more intelligent and their intelligence more prayerful.

PREPARING

1. The ideal group size is 8–10. If more people want to take part, form two groups with a leader in each one.
2. Try to meet each member of the group before the meetings start. At least, send the potential members clear information about *where* the group is going to meet, the *dates* and the *time*. Ask them to bring a notepad and pen. Stress the importance of attending every meeting.
3. Arrange for the group to meet in a warm room, with comfortable seats set out in such a way that everyone can see everyone else. The room should be large enough for people to work in pairs and sub-groups without getting in each other's way. Otherwise, there should be another room nearby that is available, such as the kitchen.
4. Provide a copy of the Study Guide for each member of the group. You will also need large sheets of paper and felt-tip pens of different colours. Check before each session what else you need: for one session you will need candles, for others bibles, hymn books and copies of the Communion Service.

BEGINNING

1. Allow two hours for each session. Always start and finish on time: this helps the group to feel secure (but see below, *Ending* 1).
2. If members of the group do not know each other, spend a few minutes making introductions. For example, ask each person to give their name, one thing they would like the group to know about them, and one reason why they have come to the group.

3. Read through each Unit yourself two or three times so that you understand it. Plan the timing of each session, making notes in the margin of your Study Guide of the amount of time you think the group will spend on each activity. For example:

Activity	*Minutes*
to do	10
to read	10
to do	a 5
	b 15
	c 40
to read	10
to do	10
to pray	8
check next session	2
	120

WORKING

1. There are five different kinds of activity:

TO DO

An exercise for the group to do, individually or together.

TO READ

A passage to read. It is best if this is read aloud so that people's speed of reading does not matter. If you are going to ask someone else to read the extracts from the Report, ask them to prepare them before the session. Some of them are not easy. Give space after the reading for people to digest what has been read, and then have a time for discussion.

TO PONDER

A short passage which is just read aloud and thought about.

TO PRAY

A period of prayer which is part of the Unit, not just an optional extra.

AT HOME

An exercise for members of the group to do in between meetings.

2. The group is asked to work in four different ways:

On your own	Members work individually on an exercise or reflect on their own on what they have just heard.
In pairs	This enables members to share their own personal material confidentially. Change the pairings each time, so that members of the group can meet and work with everyone, and then there is a real mixing of attitudes and views.
In two groups	This gives everyone a chance to get to grips with an idea more deeply, and gives more chance for everyone to say something.
In the group	The whole group discusses or works together.

3. The material in this Study Guide may seem very rich, as it engages people's experience of God, prayer and the Christian life. Discussion may go off in many directions or go deeply into one aspect. As leader you will need to be sensitive. Be flexible enough to let the group linger where it seems appropriate, despite the timetable you have set.

ENDING

1. If you feel the group would benefit by over-running by a few minutes, say so, be clear by how much, and get everyone's agreement. Try not to make a habit of it.
2. Check that everyone is clear about the date, time and place of the next meeting.
3. At the end of the final session, ask the group members to write down their reactions to both the content of the Study Guide and the way you have led it. The writers of the Study Guide welcome comments on the content: you may discover better ways of being a leader.

1 HOW CAN YOU BELIEVE IN GOD?

TO DO

As a group
Listen to this quotation from the Report:

'How are atheists produced?', asked Bernard Shaw. 'In probably nine cases out of ten, what happens is something like this. A beloved wife or husband or child or sweetheart is gnawed to death by cancer, stultified by epilepsy, struck dumb and helpless by apoplexy, or strangled by croup or diphtheria: and the looker-on, after praying vainly to God to refrain from such horrible and wanton cruelty, indignantly repudiates faith in the divine monster, and becomes not merely indifferent and sceptical, but fiercely and actively hostile to religion.' (page 17)

In pairs
Share your response to what you have just heard. What bells does it ring with your experience? What makes religious belief difficult for you? When has your faith been most severely tested and tried?

In the group
List the main areas of difficulty that have been shared in the pairs.

TO READ

And yet, in spite of it all, people go on believing. In spite of the terrible things done in the name of God and religion, in spite of divisions and disunity, people go on believing. Many of the most common problems that people have in believing are not new. They have been around for centuries. They may be expressed and argued about in different ways, but the problems are ancient.

Some people, particularly those who are 'well-off' in material terms, see no need for God. They are doing very nicely without, thank you very much. However, many people, living in different contexts, search for meaning and purpose in life. This search is expressed in various ways, but, as it is commonly said, 'People have to believe in something'.

Often this sense of 'having to believe' is related to a sense of wonder, to the birth of a baby, a beautiful sunset or falling in love. These experiences, and others, can awaken a sense of thankfulness that is very close to religious belief. It can indeed be an essential part of it.

TO DO

In pairs

1. Talk about one way in which you find meaning in life.
2. Share one experience that has made belief in God more real for you.

In the group

List the things talked about in pairs.

TO READ

Although many of the obstacles to believing in God have their roots back in history, one problem is felt to be modern. The rapid advance in scientific knowledge over the past two hundred years has made many Christians uneasy and unsure. Science seems to be dealing with certainties; belief cannot be so sure.

As time goes on, it is becoming clear that scientific knowledge is by no means as massively certain as it has been felt to be.

Reliability, to be worth having, does not have to reach a degree of absolute certainty. Very different kinds of reliability are attained in an immense variety of different enterprises. They emerge in such things as science, history, commonsense, sociology, the administration of justice, marriage, economics, orienteering, doing the pools. In some enterprises (e.g. the popular and perhaps all forms of astrology) there is no reliability at all.

Where the sciences are concerned, the constant probing and testing of reliability, generation by generation, makes them 'well-winnowed traditions'. To winnow is to sift the grain from the chaff. It is by this process of sifting and testing that the sciences become well-winnowed traditions of great reliability, while still remaining provisional, corrigible and incomplete. They can never be known to give a final account of 'how the universe really is'.

That may always lie beyond us. But they can give accounts which are highly reliable for particular purposes, and they can eliminate some other accounts. (pages 23–24)

But if this is true of science, is it equally true of theology?

It is from human experience that theology begins. It is through the created order, through signs or words, or through our relations to ourselves, our neighbours, and the circumstances of time and space in which we live that the presence of God is normally mediated. Theology, with its concepts and images, is not unlike science with its models, in that theology too seeks to explore the unknown and unobservable, not by representations, but by formulations of the divine behaviour which can then be constantly checked against experience. These theological models, whether boldly pictorial or philosophically abstract, are creative precisely because they are not literal descriptions. They are tools to enable us to think and imagine, and so to advance in our approach to truth. (page 28)

TO DO

On your own
What past pictures of God have you had which you found useful? (These pictures might be pictures you had as a child, or they might be pictures that people in the past held.) How do these pictures fit in with the view you have now of God?

Write a prayer that uses an image or picture of God that you find important and real for you now, at this stage in your life.

O PRAY

In the group
Each person prays aloud the prayer they have written.

PONDER

Listen as someone reads this passage slowly and reflectively:

The fact that those who lived in the past may have held to certain pictures or imaginations which we now know to be defective or even wrong, does not mean that they were therefore wholly wrong about everything, nor that they have nothing of value, or of judgement on us, to offer. Newton was not wholly discarded by Einstein. Indeed, Einstein addressed a famous letter to Newton in which, having pointed out why Newton's physics would no longer work for all phenomena, he suddenly pulled himself up and wrote:

> *Enough of this. Newton, forgive me. You found the only way that, in your day, was at all possible for a man of the highest powers of intellect and creativity. The concepts that you created still dominate the way we think in physics, although we now know that they must be replaced by others farther removed from the sphere of immediate experience if we want to try for a more profound understanding of the way things are interrelated.*

Christians too have their own comparable conversation with the past. We live in the Body of Christ and therefore in the communion of saints. We too can recognise that others have left a mark upon us by the prayers they have prayed, by the love they have expressed in life, by the failures for which they have needed forgiveness and have found it. This is to recognise a truth and an experience which we can trust, and on which we are entitled to rely – not uncritically, not as though it foreclosed every argument and solved every problem, but as a great foundation on which to live now for our time and in our day. It is an accumulation of irreversible gains. (pages 30–31)

HOW CAN YOU TALK ABOUT GOD? 2

TO DO

Alone
Read the following statements. Put 'o' against those you think are true for everyone, wherever they live, and 's' against those you think are true only for some people.

. . . a The sun will rise tomorrow.
. . . b When water is heated, after a time it bubbles.
. . . c Tomorrow never comes.
. . . d Eating people is wrong.
. . . e The witness said, 'They'd obviously just had a row. You could cut the atmosphere with a knife.'
. . . f My love is like a red, red rose.
. . . g God made the world.
. . . h People are a mixture of body, mind and spirit.

In the group
Share the conclusions and discuss the differences.

TO READ

Modern Western culture seems to distinguish between 'objective' language, which refers to observable realities 'out there', and 'subjective' language which refers to ideas and beliefs 'in here'. The Report explores this commonly held understanding about the ways in which people use language.

The effects of science have been felt not least in the realm of language. It has become common to assume that there are only two ways of using language. One is a literal, fact-stating use, which alone 'conveys information' about the way things are. This is the language of science and of commonsense. The other is mood-expressing, attitude-evoking language which is the domain of metaphor and myth and is not designed to carry truth: it is the language of poetry and as such 'subjective', while the other, the language of science is 'objective'. (pages 34–35)

For example, here are two ways of describing the common daffodil. One is from the botanist's point of view, the other from the poet's point of view.

1. *Narcissus pseudo-narcissus*
   Flower-stalk hollow, two edged, bearing near its summit a membranous sheath and a single flower, nectary, notched and curled at the margin, as long as the sepals and petals.

2. I wandered lonely as a cloud
   That floats on high o'er vales and hills,
   When all at once I saw a crowd,
   A host, of golden daffodils;
   Beside the lake, beneath the trees,
   Fluttering and dancing in the breeze.

   William Wordsworth

The Report goes further:

Associated with this dichotomy between factual and expressive language is another – that between public and private domains. It is tempting to draw a distinction between an area of public truth, determined by objective methods of a broadly scientific kind, and a sphere of private preference, where the only sort of truth that obtains is what is 'true for me' or 'true for you'. Religion, it is widely felt, belongs to the latter realm. It is an essentially private matter to do with individuals and their personal feelings. This notion reinforces the conviction that many people have that religion has no part to play in the corporate life of a society. (pages 35–36)

So in our culture there seems to be two types of language:

A	B
Objective	Subjective
Literal	Mood-expressing
Fact-stating	Attitude evoking
Information conveying	Metaphorical
Scientific	To do with myth
Commonsense	Poetic
Factual	Expressive
Public	Private

In the group
Recite together the *Apostles' Creed*:

I believe in God the Father Almighty, Maker of heaven and earth: And in Jesus Christ his only Son our Lord, Who was conceived by the Holy Ghost, Born of the Virgin Mary, Suffered under Pontius Pilate, Was crucified, dead, and buried, He descended into hell; The third day he rose again from the dead, He ascended into heaven, And sitteth on the right hand of God the Father Almighty; From thence he shall come to judge the quick and the dead. I believe in the Holy Ghost; The holy Catholick Church; The Communion of Saints; The Forgiveness of sins; The Resurrection of the body, And the Life everlasting. Amen.

Alone
Which of the statements of the Creed can be described under the type of language A, and which under type B?

In the group
Share your conclusions, noting the agreements and disagreements.

Close examination makes this distinction between 'objective' and 'subjective' language difficult to hold. The scientist, who is thought to be investigating 'realities out there' actually uses metaphorical language ('ideas in here') in the attempt to comprehend and communicate those realities.

It seems to be a basic propensity of the human mind to extend its knowledge by the use of the imagination, endeavouring to form images or models of the way things might be, and then testing the hypothesis in the appropriate manner. The reason why metaphor plays the part it does in scientific discourse is precisely because it is the equivalent in language of thinking with models. (page 40)

Even though this is seen to be true of the way in which scientists use language, there is a tendency to dismiss the language of metaphor and model when used by the poet as purely 'subjective' and 'mood-evoking' and, therefore, not about 'realities out there'. However, if metaphor and model are used by the scientist to comprehend and communicate 'realities out there', it follows that the poet can use that kind of language in the same way, that is to refer to 'realities out there' as well as 'ideas in here'.

Unlike the scientist, the poet is not, as a rule, concerned to generalise and analyse, but rather to describe what is individual and unique, whether it be an abstract idea or a particular thing. In the case of both the scientist and the poet, the use of comparisons both extends the scope of possible understanding and brings what is described into clearer focus. (page 39)

The two types of language overlap, as can be seen clearly in the ways in which some poets and some scientists have described their methods of working. A poet will often have the idea of a poem intuitively, 'in a flash', but then can follow hours, if not days, of hard work. The poet *experiments* with words until the exact sense is conveyed, and the whole poem 'sounds right'. Similarly, some of the most famous scientific discoveries begin not with an experiment, but with an incident that makes a scientist say, 'I wonder why?' or 'I wonder if . . . ?' Then follow the hours, days, weeks or even years of *experiment*.

So 'God-talk' cannot be dismissed as 'subjective', only about 'ideas in here', and therefore about private truth. It is also an attempt, by use of metaphor and model, to comprehend and communicate 'realities out there'. Within Christian belief, in the language of the Bible and the Creeds, of hymns and prayers, 'objective' language and 'subjective' language are bound together. Christians may disagree about the boundary between the two. That does not mean that people need claim that the one is 'true' and the other 'false', the one 'public' and the other 'private'.

TO PONDER

Alone

Go back over the two 'TO DO's. Would you respond in the same way if you were to do them again?

PRAY

Say together:
God be in my head
  and in my understanding;
God be in my eyes,
  and in my looking;
God be in my mouth,
  and in my speaking;
God be in my heart,
  and in my thinking;
God be at my end,
  and at my departing.

HOME

Go through some hymns for Christmas and Passiontide and explore how they use 'objective' and 'subjective' language. How do you distinguish between the two?

3 THE GOD OF THE BIBLE

TO DO

Alone
Using what you can remember from the Bible, if you can, make a list of up to *ten* answers to the question, 'What is God like?' Against each answer, try to note the biblical passage(s) that lie(s) behind it – not the references, a description will do.

In the group
Compare the lists. How different are they? How many biblical passages seem to be mentioned in all?

TO READ

Imagine that all the Bibles in the world were destroyed. Along with them went all the books that had any quotations from the Bible. The Church would no longer be able to go back to the written word, but would have to rely on the memories of those who had heard it read, Sunday after Sunday, or who had read it every day in their Bible Study.

But no one person's memory – unless they had learned the whole Bible by heart – would be enough. Everyone would remember different passages, perhaps their favourite ones. One story, for example, may have been very important to someone at a time of personal tragedy. Someone else might treasure a passage told by a favourite Sunday School teacher. However, if everyone contributed from their memory, the total picture would be far more complete.

The situation is, of course, entirely imaginary. But it is not so very different from the ways in which much of the Bible came into being. The Bible came out of the life of a worshipping community, much of it existing in oral form before it was written down. The Bible began in people's memories as they told and retold the stories that were important for their community.

Often, the picture of God that came out of these stories was not consistent. At times, one picture seemed to contradict another. That did not matter, as long as *all* the stories were preserved. They then balanced each other. The truths about God cannot be expressed in any other way.

DO

In the group
Go back to the list from the first TO DO in this unit. Were some of the answers contradictory?

READ

The Biblical writings are the product, not simply of individual authors, but of communities.

It can never have been true to the nature of Scripture to regard it solely as the medium through which a succession of uniquely inspired writers has conveyed the truth about God to later generations, even though such writers, named or unnamed, must have played a crucial part. Scripture is also, and perhaps chiefly, the distillation of those perceptions of the reality of God which came to a worshipping community under the impact of particular historical events, of the genius of legislators, prophets and thinkers, and finally of the encounter with Jesus himself. This in turn tells us something of immense importance about God: that God is known, primarily and characteristically, in the shared worship, experience and reflection of men and women who meet in his name and serve him in the world. (pages 53–54)

The characteristic way in which the Bible communicates its ideas is by stories or narrative. More than half of both Testaments consists of 'what happened'.

To say that God is revealed in story in the Bible is to say something about God himself. It is a clue to the power of God to influence the human heart. Few people are led to belief in God by reading books of speculative theology, but many owe their faith in good measure to stories – not only the stories of the Bible, but the stories told by novelists and poets and perhaps above all the stories told by their friends. What is the 'testimony' which to many Christians is so significant if not one person's story of his or her own life, interpreted in the light of faith, and challenging the hearer, 'This happened to me; it can also happen to you?' (pages 55–56)

'What happened' has come to be understood at different levels. There is 'what happened' on the surface, but there is also 'what was going on' underneath. It is this 'what was going on underneath' that gives such significance to the stories people hear.

The stories about the God of the Bible tell of a being who acts in many ways. There is often tension between these ways. The danger is that people see only those ways that 'fit' their particular understanding. The Bible refuses to let people be so one-sided.

An example is the traditional portrayal of God by means of models or attributes derived from the activities and the attitudes of men rather than women. The Bible offers a wider range of attributes. God is occasionally described in terms of tenderness and long-suffering vigilance usually thought more appropriate to motherhood than fatherhood. Our own generation, with its concern for the equality of the sexes, invites fresh attention to this aspect of the biblical tradition, so that the richness of Scripture's perception of God may enlarge our imagining to press beyond our own restricted models and categories of gender towards the ultimate mystery of God. (page 58)

Another question raised by the amount of story in the Bible is 'Is it true?' The relationship of the biblical stories to historical events is complex.

Although there is good reason to believe that the story of God's involvement in the affairs of his people and of the world is firmly rooted in historical fact, we have to recognise that the actual telling of the story, if it is to bring out the significance and implications of this involvement, may depart at times from the strictly factual reporting expected of scientific historians. This again tells us something of importance about God. If he can legitimately be represented as an actor in and influence upon the course of history, the nature of this action and influence is too subtle and varied always to be adequately expressed in objective historical statement. (pages 59–60)

Scientists use 'models' to describe the physical universe. Corrections do not necessarily make those models wrong; they can still be used as a guide (Look back to pages 3–4, TO

PONDER). In the same way, the 'models' used in the Bible to describe God are open to correction.

In the faith of Christians, Jesus Christ himself represents the most radical 'correction' of ideas about God that the world has ever known. In him there is a finality and authority such that no comparable correction is to be expected again within human history. He does not necessarily invalidate all that is said about God in the Old Testament, or even in other world religions. But by his suffering, death and resurrection he significantly enlarges the range of human experience which can be 'read' as a testimony to the love and the power of God; and in his teaching he offers new 'models' of understanding which go far beyond what was available before. (pages 66–67)

The very nature of the Bible's witness to God – its basis in the experience of a community, its emphasis on speaking about him in historical narrative, and so forth – allows us to form certain conclusions about God, and also to expect a certain consistency in the descriptions of his character. But the inadequacy of language to encompass so great a reality must prevent us from achieving a perfectly systematic account of biblical theology, and warn us that any one account of the biblical evidence is likely to need correction (without thereby becoming obsolete) in the light of new perceptions and methods. (page 67)

Choose one or two of these exercises:

1. *In pairs* What would you want to say to someone who asked you, 'is the Bible true?'
   In the group Discuss what the pairs came up with.
2. *In pairs* 'Tell me what God is like'. You can give a reply using five passages from the Bible. Which five would you choose?
   In the group Compare the passages the pair chose, and their reasons for choosing them.
3. *In the group* Go through the Communion Service, picking out the biblical stories or passages that lie behind or are explicitly quoted in the different parts of the service.

Spend some minutes in silence reflecting on what has come out of the exercises. Then say together:

TO PRAY

O God, you have given us in the Bible a record of your dealings with human beings in times past. Help us so to understand that record, that we, in our turn and in our day, can come to know you and understand how you work in the world. We ask this in the name of Jesus.

Or make up your own prayer to express what has been discussed in this Unit. Then pray the prayers in the group.

THE GOD OF JESUS 4

Read the following passage from the Report:

The God of Jesus is the God of the Old Testament, personally involved in his creation, holy and one. In him justice and love are held together. His ultimate triumph over evil is sure. Through his Spirit he is the author of all zeal for goodness in humankind. His ears are open to the prayers of his servants, who can speak to him in their hearts. (page 85)

Many of the attitudes or ideas that people hold are based on what they gained from their parents. These can range from the pub in which people drink to the newspaper they read, from the political party that they vote for to the car that they drive.

Alone
Draw a shield, and divide it into four. In each quarter draw a symbol to represent one idea or belief that you have inherited from your parents or your family or your birthplace. Underneath the shield, write your 'motto', the saying which you remember your mother or father saying to you most often.

In pairs
Share your shield, explaining why you have put in what you have put in.

In the group
Share any reflections you may have about the whole exercise. Has it been worthwhile?

TO READ

'You're just like your father' or 'You're just like your mother' may be compliments or insults. It may be something about someone's opinions, or their generosity, or the angle of their spine. Often people are 'chips off the old block' in a variety of ways that cannot be explained merely by the genes. The beliefs and opinions of parents so often form the basis from which people start their thinking.

In later life, some may try to rethink everything through from the beginning. Even that will be done against the background of their basic assumptions and pre-suppositions, some of them so fundamental that people do not even recognise that they are there.

In so-called 'primitive' societies, like those of the Bushmen or the original inhabitants of Australia, this dependence on the knowledge of parents or the tribe is literally a matter of life or death. That is how vital information about the places to find water or food is passed on. Even in the complexity of modern society the passing on of knowledge and ideas is important. We stand on the shoulders of those who have gone before us and so can see just that bit further. And so it was with Jesus. He learned from Mary and Joseph and the local synagogue about the Judaism of his time. He started with their idea of God; he started with what he had received.

By reading the gospels carefully, it is possible to discover what it was that Jesus received. At the same time, it is possible to see what were the main emphases in the Judaism of Jesus' time.

TO DO

In two sub-groups
Group A reads Luke 4.14–21: Group B reads Luke 7.18–27. Each sub-group studies its passages carefully, and makes a list of the various strands and teaching within it. Try to answer the question, 'What expectations and hopes did Jesus' hearers have if that was what he said and did?'

In the group
Share the findings of the two sub-groups.

There were four overwhelming factors essential to Jewish teaching at the time of Jesus:

TO READ

a. *First, the centrality of the Law in Jewish religion had been greatly enhanced. At a time when God's power and otherness were dramatically magnified, there was a danger that his greatness and purity might place him altogether beyond the reach of human littleness and sinfulness. But because the transcendent God was imminent in the Law, love for God could be expressed in love for the Law, and attention to its detailed demands could ensure that a person was in right relationship with God. The Law was not only central to worship, but touched people at every point in their daily lives.*

b. *Secondly, the troubled times had led many devout people to seek for visionary experiences which would reveal God's will for his people, and so bring reassurance. They hoped to penetrate the secrets of Heaven and to determine the divine plan for the future. Such experiences implied a direct knowledge of God and his will, comparable to the inspiration of the Old Testament prophets. This carried with it the danger of conflict with those who held that the Law was the sole repository of the revealed knowledge of God.*

c. *A third feature of the times is the expectation of a Messiah. Many were convinced that God would soon intervene in history to establish his own rule everlastingly. The era of justice and freedom would come only by the act of God in fulfilment of his age-long promises. But how would that act be mediated? Would it be by the political activism of the Zealots, who saw themselves as under solemn obligation to free the land from foreign rule? Or were the devout called not to act themselves, but only to 'look for the consolation of Israel'? The Pharisees, who were opposed to political activism but shared the hope of the Messiah, encouraged patient waiting for God to intervene in his own good time. The visionary literature in general (the product of the experiences mentioned in 'b.') saw God's action in cosmic rather than in political terms, though it implied that this action would not be long delayed.*

d. *The notion of the resurrection of the dead constituted a fourth point of importance in the faith of Judaism at the time of Jesus. In the Old Testament the state of the dead is virtually non-existence, cut off from the joy of the presence of Yahweh. By New Testament times, however, most Jews had come to believe in a future state in which the injustices of earthly life are done away. In the teaching of the Pharisees, rewards and punishments after death became the sanctions of moral teaching. God was seen as the judge who weighs the life of an individual to see how far he has met the demands of the Law. Thus Judaism affirms that God's sovereignty extends to the dead as well as to the living, so that the righteous of every generation are destined to have their share in the everlasting kingdom. (pages 79–81)*

TO DO

In the group
Compare the four points with the findings of the two sub-groups in the previous TO DO.

There are things in the two passages not covered by the four points. Are these examples relevant for today?

TO PRAY

In five minutes of silence reflect on what has been discussed.

In the group
Listen as one person reads the following prayer:

Eternal God, who though long ages
  prepared the way for the coming of Christ;
we praise you for your word through the prophets
  who spoke in your name,
and for all the experience and discipline of life
  that made the world long for a Saviour.
We praise you that when the time was ready Jesus came,
  as Man among humans,
  as Saviour from sin,
  as Lord of life,
  and Conqueror of death.

Help us to welcome Him into our lives,
and in the life of the world,
and so to praise you more and more
in the words that He Himself taught us.

from *New Every Morning*

Our Father . . . .

5 THE GOD OF THE DISCIPLES

TO READ

Read the following passage from the Report:

The coming of Christ brought a new realisation to the disciples of God's accessibility, a recognition of his entrance into human suffering and of his relationship to his people, and at the same time a new estimate of the person of Christ and of the Spirit in relation to God himself. (page 101)

TO DO

Alone

Select a person or an idea that is special to you. Draw a 'diagram' of the history of your relationship with the person or the idea. Put in

how the relationship started,
how it grew,
significant happenings in the relationship,
how the relationship looks now with the help of hindsight.

In pairs

Share your diagram and talk about it. What have you learnt from this exercise?

TO READ

'The penny dropped and suddenly everything made sense.' Sometimes things happen gradually, but often it is possible to look back and see that there was a turning point in a relationship with a person or the understanding of an idea.

From then on there is no going back. Things can never be the same again.

Many people have heard of Newton, Einstein, Darwin, Marx and Freud, but would perhaps be hard put to say precisely what they did or what they discovered. Yet the world of today is radically different because of them and their work. So important and far-reaching are their discoveries and insights that some of the implications are still being worked out. With some of them, their real significance is such that, as Mao Tse-tung, the Chinese Communist leader, once said when asked about the fruits of the French Revolution of 1789, 'It's too early to say'.

Jesus posed the same problems for Judaism. There were those who could not see that he was the Messiah, and so rejected him. For Jesus' disciples, 'the penny dropped'. He was the Messiah. In the light of all that Jesus did, and especially in the light of the resurrection, they saw the writings of the Old Testament in a new way. Their perception of God could never be the same again.

With the coming of Jesus Christ the Creator is made especially accessible to his creatures. But there was also a new and developing appreciation of the kind *of God who has come in the Son. For example, John's portrait of Jesus and the enfleshed Word of God, who came from the Father (John 10.30,16.28) and lived among us (1.14) represents a profound understanding of incarnation, and one which was to have a far-reaching effect on subsequent Christian doctrine. But it also contains implications for the Christian view of God himself, whose sovereign purpose 'that the world might be saved' (3.17) was brought about, John shows us, by means of a total self-giving love. The exact quality of that love was manifested in his only Son, crucified and glorified (3.13–17). (page 97)*

That is one example among many in the New Testament of the attempts to explore the significance of the coming of Jesus.

The beginnings of Christian doctrine in the New Testament are varied and tentative, and it remained for the Church Fathers to work out the implications of them. But the Christian doctrine of God is not a speculative theory. It is an attempt at understanding a profound religious experience, centred in the life and teaching of Jesus. It is an experience which is superbly captured in the words of Paul's greeting at the close of 2 Corinthians (13.14): 'The grace of the Lord Jesus Christ and the love of God and the fellowship of the Holy Spirit be with you all.' (pages 102–103)

The disciples' experience of the life and teaching of Jesus, and above all the resurrection, was decisive, but there is a real sense in which it is still too early to say just how significant it was. The implications of it are still percolating through the life of the Church.

In the New Testament, the struggle is there for all to see. In the letter to the Galatians, there is a great declaration of faith: 'There is no such thing as Jew or Greek, slave and free man, male and female; for you are all one person in Christ Jesus' (3.28). Yet in other places in the New Testament there is evidence of enormous divisions of race, class and sex in the early Church. They struggled and wrestled with what they had been given, to understand what it meant in their context, and so how they ought to behave.

That struggle still goes on.

TO DO

1. *In the group*
   List some of the issues in the life of society today. How do they compare with the issues that the New Testament is struggling with?
2. *In pairs*
   Discuss where the struggle to understand more fully the implications of what Jesus said and did is going on today
   (a) in the life of your church
   (b) in your own life

In the group
Share some of the insights of the pairs.

TO PRAY

Say together:

Lord Jesus Christ
you have revealed yourself to us,
and in this way have revealed your Father also.
But our hearts and minds are slow to believe in love.
Open us, Lord, to the wonder of your manhood;
stir us to the following of your example;
urge us to the realisation of your life here on earth in terms of our living,
that we may truly live for our fellow human beings,
and so live for you,
our God for ever and ever.

from *New Every Morning*

6 PRAYER: GOD AS TRINITY

TO DO

In the group
Sit round a lighted candle, with the lights dimmed or off. Spend *five minutes* in silence looking at the candle, paying the most careful attention to it, noticing everything you can about it.

In pairs
Share the experience you had while doing the exercise.

TO READ

Looking at a candle may seem to be a strange exercise. People's experiences while they were doing it may have been very different. Some may have found it hard to concentrate on the flame for more than a few seconds; others may have been fascinated by the many different parts of the flame. Others may have discovered that as they looked at the flame with total concentration they found themselves drawn into it, finding it difficult to separate themselves from it.

The same experience can be found in many activities where close attention is paid to something. When people are totally concentrating on what they are doing, the time passes so quickly that when they stop they are amazed. They have become absorbed in what they have been doing, drawn into it. People have been taken out of themselves. 'I don't know what came over me.'

The experience of listening to someone talking or sitting by their bedside when they are seriously ill can evoke similar feelings.

None of these experiences are 'religious' in the narrow sense of the word, and yet they are similar to the experience that people describe when they are trying to pay the same close attention to God as a conscious activity, a waiting upon God in silence.

What is it that Christians who attend silently to God discover? We are not talking of some 'contemplative' elite, but of anyone who spends even a very short time in quiet waiting upon God. Often, it must be admittied, what will be encountered is darkness, obscurity and distraction. It is no wonder that the experience has such a strange lack of obvious content, for the relationship is one unlike any other, one that relates those who pray to that without which they would not be in being at all. It is a relationship of 'absolute dependence'. Yet perhaps, amid the obscurity, a little more may be said. Usually it dawns bit by bit on the person praying that this activity, which at first seems all one's own doing, is actually the activity of another. It is the experience of being 'prayed in', the discovery that 'we do not know how to pray as we ought', but are graciously caught up in a divine conversation, passing back and forth in and through the one who prays, 'the Spirit himself bearing witness with our spirit'. We come to prayer empty-handed, aware of weakness, inarticulacy and even of a certain hollow 'fear and trembling', yet it is precisely in these conditions that the divine dialogue flows. Here then is a way of beginning to understand what it might be to talk of the distinctiveness of the Spirit. (pages 107–108)

In allowing the divine activity of prayer to happen, the one who prays begins to glimpse what it might be to be 'in Christ' or to 'have the mind of Christ', or to be 'fellow heirs with Christ'. It is to allow oneself to be shaped by the mutual interaction of Father and Spirit; and in praying the prayer of Christ, in letting the Spirit cry 'Abba, Father', to make the transition from regarding Christ merely as an external model for imitation to entering into his divine life itself. Paul does not idly say, 'It is no longer I who live, but Christ who lives in me'. To discover this posture of prayer is to be remodelled by the activity of God in the redeemed life of 'sonship'. It is to become nothing less than 'other Christs' in the particularity of our lives, not by any active merit of our own, but simply by willing that which already holds us in existence to reshape us in the likeness of his Son. (page 109)

TO DO

Alone
Read these passages again silently, picking out phrases or sentences that seem to speak particularly to you. How far do the passages match your experience of prayer?

In pairs
Tell each other what you feel in response to the passages.

In the group
Share, in turn, one feeling you have had about the passages, and how it relates to your experience of prayer.

TO READ

Prayer is an activity in which Christians encounter God. This experience has been common to all Christians in every generation. So the experience of today's Christians matches the experiences of earlier generations who struggled to describe this God whom they encountered. Out of their experience, they tried to find the words to talk about God, tried to do theology – literally 'God talk' – that did justice to that experience. Some of those words can be found in the creeds. It is a mistake to think of creeds as dry and dusty word-play without remembering the activities and the experiences out of which the words came.

TO DO

In the group
Look at the *Nicene Creed* (the one used in the Anglican Communion Service). Does the discussion in this Unit throw any light on the language of the creed as it tries to describe the relationship between Father, Son and Spirit?

In pairs
Whom do you pray to? Does this say anything about how you think of God as Father, Son and Spirit?

TO PRAY

Leader: The Spirit enables us to recognise the Son, and with him worship the father.
The Spirit of the Lord is with you.
Response: And with thy spirit.

Spend five minutes in silent prayer, and end by singing or saying the hymn, 'Come Holy Ghost, our souls inspire'.

AT HOME

Reflect on these two passages from the Report:

Councils concerned with faith in the Trinity were not periodic bureaucratic reviews of a continuing theoretical problem, but were urgently called to meet passionate demands. What was the source of this passion? Why did it manifest itself only rarely in academic circles but all too frequently at congregational level, in the gossip of the court, or in banter over the shop counter? Were all the Lord's people theologians? Or was their argument about their own experience of God as Trinity, and the variety of interpretations of this experience? (page 113)

Most professing Christians know how to use the language of Father, Son and Spirit in the varied and unsystematic way that we find in the New Testament. There are 'rules' for this language that are generally acknowledged in the Church. What many perhaps do not realise is that efficiency in operating the 'rules' of this New Testament language is still a very far cry from acknowledgement of God as Trinity. (pages 104–105)

PRAYER: GOD IN US 7

TO DO

Alone
Think of the times in your life when you have not 'wanted to be alone with yourself'.

In pairs
Share one of those experiences with your partner.

TO READ

'Silence is golden' but it is hard to find silence today. Even a vantage point on a remote hill will still be within range of the nearest main road or a passing aeroplane. At home, the radio or the television is constantly on to provide some background noise.

Perhaps this generation is less able than its predecessors to bear silence. People do not like to be reminded that they are 'on their own', and will do anything to make that aloneness more bearable. That makes the unavoidable times of aloneness – the middle of the night, before an operation, after bereavement – even more difficult.

It is at those times that memories come flooding back of things that were done or words that were said. It is at those times that people feel ashamed, regretful, or just plain miserable.

The description by those Christians who spend time 'in quiet waiting upon God' is similar.

The God whom Christians meet in this prayer is one who appears, sometimes for very long periods, to desert us; or worse still to press upon us with apparently negative pressure, causing disturbance, deep uneasiness, the highlighting of sin and even the fear of insanity. If we take our cue from the agony in the garden or from the dereliction of the cross, then the authentic cry of 'Abba' indicates that the most powerful and active presence of God is mysteriously compatible with the all too human experiences of anxiety and desolation. (pages 109–110)

Equally significant in its 'incarnational' implications is the disconcerting discovery in this kind of prayer that the God who acts in us wants us whole, conscious and unconscious, soul and body. It is truly an effect of this prayer that we are gradually forced to accept and integrate those dark and repressed strands of the unconscious that we would rather not acknowledge, and along with these, all aspects of our sexuality, both bodily and emotional. (page 110)

In prayer, God shows himself. One effect may be that people are shown a more complete picture of themselves. With this greater self-awareness comes the ability to see and hear more, more of the 'divine conversation' within God and more of how this conversation is made with the whole of humanity and the whole of creation.

To find ourselves 'in Christ' is gradually to break through the limitations of the individualism and introspection that often characterise prayer in its earliest stages. For all prayer has its corporate dimension; and to pray 'in Christ' is to perceive the flow of trinitarian love coursing out to encompass the whole of humanity. The whole creation, inanimate as well as animate, is taken up in this trinitarian flow. (pages 110–111)

TO DO

Alone
Slowly re-read these passages from the Report. Do the ideas match your experience of prayer or not?

Make a note of anything you want to say to God in response to these ideas.

TO READ

Prayer provides the opportunity for the Christian to join in the 'divine conversation'. The experience of prayer is never and was never a 'private affair'. In meeting to worship together, the members of the early churches experienced the richness of prayer and used it to inform their descriptions of God, which remain valid for today.

The public prayer of the church allowed considerable opportunity to the congregation for being receptive, for listening and for being 'prayed in'. Congregations at the liturgy for the first four centuries were for the most part silent. People simply allowed themselves to be caught up in the flow of the eucharistic action, which was felt by them to unite heaven and earth and to bring them through Christ by the Holy Spirit to the Father. (page 114)

The services provided the opportunity and continue to provide the opportunity for invoking and joining the 'divine conversation'. The experience of worshipping together at the Eucharist reinforces the sense of relatedness, of dialogue, that belongs to the very nature of God.

TO PRAY

In silence, refer to your 'note' to God from the last TO DO. If you have something that you want to pray aloud, use the space in the following sequence.

Leader: The Spirit of the Lord is with you.
Response: And with thy spirit.

After any short prayers have been offered, spend five minutes in silent prayer.

End by singing or saying the hymn, 'Come, Holy Ghost, our souls inspire'.

TO PONDER

If then it is the experience of prayer, both personal and corporate, which is our primary access to God as Trinity, several important conclusions accrue for today.

First, we must become aware that prayer must have priority . . .

Secondly, the experience of being mysteriously caught up by divine dialogue into the likeness of Christ will never in itself yield hard-edged conceptual certainty . . .

Thirdly, light may be thrown on Christianity's relation to other world religions. For the obscurity, the darkness, the sheer defencelessness of wordless prayer usually lead to a greater openness to other religions than to an assured sense of superiority.

Fourthly, an approach to the Trinity through prayer has implications for the currently vexed issue of masculine and feminine language as applied to God. The 'masculine' and 'feminine' qualities (as we call them) which we all share in varying admixture are both of them for us clues and glimpses of the wholeness of divine life and love. (page 118–121)

THE GOD WHO CALLS: OBEDIENCE IN PRAYER 8

TO DO

In pairs
Share any experience you have had in which you have felt your life to have been taken over. Can you recall an event, or a person or a sudden insight which has changed you?

TO READ

A common feature of being a human being is that for much of the time, life is humdrum. It is possible to see what is going to happen. People feel in control and at the centre of their lives.

Every now and again, things happen which change everything: a sudden idea lights up new areas; falling in love transforms everything and everybody. What makes these kinds of experience special? One common feature is the way the person becomes the object of the experience, rather than the subject. The experience comes to them uninvited. 'It came to me out of the blue.' 'Suddenly I was struck by . . .' This sort of experience calls for a response.

It should be clear by now that believing in God is different from believing in any other truth and that knowing God is not quite like knowing anything else. There are several reasons why this must be so, and one of them is that God is essentially and forever the Initiator and the Animator. He can never for a moment be simply the object of our thought or our knowing or our believing. In some way he is always the prompter of our search for him, the director of our speculation about him, the giver of our faith in him. There is no understanding of God which is not by his self-revelation. Yet he brings this about without infringing the freedom of our relationship with him or emasculating the part we play in it; and one method by which he achieves this is that of call and response, a theme which runs through the whole Bible. People, both individually and corporately, experience God as the One who calls at a particular time and with a specific demand. Individually or corporately they are free to respond or to refuse. (*page 122*)

We are indeed as free to accept or dissent from statements about God as to obey or resist his commands. But it is in the process of obedience that a learning takes place far deeper and more personal than the mental acceptance of propositions, because it is not just a learning but a loving. In the words of the ancient tag, 'God is known in proportion as he is loved'. (*page 123*)

The divine call does indeed, for those who respond to it, have something irresistible about it, but their response is like that of a poet to the Muse, or of a lover to the beloved, or of a free people to the call to withstand tyranny. In our response to God's call there is a strong element of 'We can do no other'. (*page 123*)

TO DO

Alone
Re-read the passages to yourself. Have you had any experience that in any way matches this account of being called by God? How did you respond?

TO READ

Having the will to do God's will means something more specific than 'I will be good'. Even if it is only crossing the road to take responsibility for someone else's need, it involves a change of direction, and perseverance in some venture of which the limits are not yet defined. This is how 'willing to do the will' becomes a discovery of God. (*page 124*)

The 'willing to do the will' by which we come to the knowledge of God need not involve anything dramatic or devastating. But however small-scale and mundane the divine commands may be, our response will involve us in some kind of break-out from a routine. (*page 125*)

These passages are very clear about the human response to God's call. It involves change: change of direction, breaking routines, changes willingly made. It involves decision and action, efforts of the will. 'Obedience' can be used to describe this response. It is not, in the present culture, a popular word. Yet understood in this way it leads to freedom and creativity and deeper understanding of God.

Races are won and concerts performed only by athletes and musicians whose achievements are built on hours and days and years of practice undertaken by huge effort of will. It is a process that changes the person and changes and deepens the understanding. Obedience is doing, and not simply thinking or talking. Jesus says he came to *do* the will of the Father who sent him.

So what is the Christian to do?

Most people who pray begin to do so in simple obedience. They are called or taught to pray – whether in their childhood home, or at the time of confirmation or conversion, or through a personal experience of challenge, bewilderment or need. (page 126)

The practice of prayer leads to increasing breadth and comprehensiveness in the range of prayer, to a growing sense that every facet of ourselves may and should be exposed to God in prayer and every aspect of the world's life laid before him. (page 127)

TO DO

In pairs
Tell your partner how you were taught to pray and what you find most difficult about your prayer.

In the group
Make a list of the difficulties that the group has with prayer. What seem to be the most common ones?

TO READ

The report describes these areas of difficulty that people find as they obey the call in prayer:

Some people find that, instead of saying to God first 'sorry' and then 'thank you' and then 'please', as they were taught to in childhood, they need to say all three things at the very same time, so that the precise content of their prayer cannot be expressed in words or even identified in thought. Thus they find themselves reduced to an inarticulate silence. (page 128)

There is the difficulty – met at some time by almost all who pray – caused by 'unanswered' prayer. This may lead in a quite simple and direct way to a larger or deeper understanding of God. One prays for the particular and, although the particular does not come to pass, something does come to pass which shows the particular in a different light and alters one's attitude to it. So the practice of prayer moves away from *any aspiration to influence the will of God into conformity with our own, and* towards *the aspiration to align our own will more closely with whatever may be the will of God. (pages 129–130)*

Another difficulty is the experience in prayer of distress, darkness and pain. The total exposure of oneself in prayer can be almost a breaking apart of oneself; prayer for a suffering world may leave one appalled by that suffering; the 'approachable' God to whom one began to pray may seem to withdraw himself and leave one disregarded and abandoned. Those who are led along the road of obedience into pain and darkness may find themselves discovering, so to speak, 'what it is like' to be the God who is revealed in Christ crucified and come to understand a dimension of the being of God which previously was hidden from them. (page 129)

TO DO

Alone
Think about your difficulties in prayer in the context of the passages you have just read.

Think of one thing that has surprised you, one thing that has reassured you and one thing that you have learned in the passages or in the discussion.

In the group
1. Share those things in the group
2. Discuss how you can act on these discoveries

TO PRAY

In silence, read the *Our Father*, slowly and prayerfully,

Our Father, who art in heaven,
hallowed be thy name;
thy kingdom come;
thy will be done;
on earth as it is in heaven.

Give us this day our daily bread.
And forgive us our trespasses,
as we forgive them that trespass against us.
And lead us not into temptation:
but deliver us from evil.
For thine is the kingdom, the power, and the glory, for ever and ever. Amen.

Now say the *Our Father* together aloud.

TO PONDER

'Thy will be done,' is not a word of acquiescence said with a gesture of helplessness nor a comment on the unavoidable. It does not mean 'May thy will be passively suffered'. It means 'May thy will be accomplished, wrought out'. God's will is to be done on earth in the same manner in which it is done in heaven. *(page 130)*

9 THE GOD WHO CALLS: OBEDIENCE IN SERVICE

TO DO

Alone
Complete three sentences, each of which begins with 'A Christian is someone who . . .'

In the group
List the ways in which people have completed their sentences.

Listen while someone reads:

To the average person the embodiment of 'real Christianity' is the Good Samaritan. Here is one who devotes himself to the service of human need – without regard to the origin, race, class or character of the wounded man or to anything else except the fact that he is a 'neighbour' (i.e. that he is 'near by') and that he is in need: and here is one whom Jesus used as a direct and pointed example to his followers: 'Go and do likewise'. (page 131)

TO READ

When someone is described as a 'real Christian', nine times out of ten it will be because they are directly and personally involved in meeting a need or needs of those around them. They are seen to be obeying Jesus' command, 'Go and do likewise'. Often in these situations it is not just the needy who receive a service; in giving, the good neighbour can also receive and be blessed. Something seems to happen which may be described as an experience of the Kingdom of God.

There are two areas in particular where direct personal involvement is called for urgently. It is called for in the large cities where there is so much loneliness and isolation. It is also called for in raising money to help feed the world's starving. But this is not enough.

There is another manner of Christian obedience which is essential if the situation of the poor and oppressed is to be radically transformed in the long term – the indirect manner of pressing and working for political, economic and social reform.

Those who advocate this manner of obedience would not deny the importance of the traditional manner in certain circumstances. They would not suggest that the Good Samaritan should have left the traveller to die, and set off to campaign for better policing of the roads. However preoccupation with a need that can be directly met may blind us to the real need which cannot be directly met – the need for justice, a fair wage or equality of opportunity. In the seats of power, personal kindness may actually diminish awareness of the oppressiveness and even cruelty of one's lifestyle and social role.

One might say that the varieties of human need can be gathered into two broad categories – the need for love which can best be met by direct and personal action and the need for justice which can best be met by indirect and political action. What is essential is the recognition that both the traditional manner of response to human need and the political manner are manners or methods of obedience. Both contain moral dangers and ambiguities; but both at their best can be honest and obedient responses to Christ's command, 'Go and do likewise'. (page 132–133)

TO DO

1. *In the group* Discuss the previous passages, answering the questions:

   Which is my characteristic manner or method of obedience?

   What would happen if I also acted in the other manner?

2. *In two sub-groups*

   Group A List the things that are being done voluntarily in your community. Where are the gaps in the service and the care? Can you do anything about them?

   Group B List the major injustices that you see in this society and in the world. Where are people trying to do something about them? How?

   In the group

   Discuss the suggestions made by both groups.

TO PRAY

On your own:
Reflect on Jesus' command, 'Go and do likewise'.
Give thanks for all that is being done, in your community and wider.
Pray for all that needs to be done.

In the group
Listen to this reading:

The meaning of the great Vision of Judgement in Matthew's Gospel (25.31–46) has gone deep into Christian poetry and imagery. 'The poor of the world are my body, said he.' Christ incognito is ever at hand, serving and to be served. 'Inasmuch as you did it to one of the least of these my brothers, you did it to me.' Is not all such compassion, in Paul's phrase, a 'discerning of the body', that body of humanity into which by birth came the Son of Man, thereby made like to his brethren? For the purpose of the parable, the knowing was in the doing even if awareness was first wanting. 'Lord, when did we see you *sick?' Within the answered imperative of compassion was the secret of the divine presence. (pages 145–146)*

After a silent pause, end by saying together,

> And I heard the voice of the Lord saying,
> 'Whom shall I send and who will go for us?'
> Then I said 'Here am I! Send me!'
> (Isaiah 6.8)

PONDER

'But seek the welfare of the city where I have sent you into exile, and pray to the Lord on its behalf, for in its welfare you will find your welfare.'

Jeremiah 29.7

10 THE GOD IN WHOM WE TRUST

TO DO

In the group
Listen while someone reads the quotation with which this study course began:

'How are atheists produced?', asked Bernard Shaw. 'In probably nine cases out of ten, what happens is something like this. A beloved wife or husband or child or sweetheart is gnawed to death by cancer, stultified by epilepsy, struck dumb and helpless by apoplexy, or strangled by croup or diphtheria: and the looker-on, after praying to God to refrain from such horrible and wanton cruelty, indignantly repudiates faith in the divine monster, and becomes not merely indifferent and sceptical, but fiercely and actively hostile to religion.' *(page 17)*

In pairs
If you were the looker-on, what question would you want to ask about God?

In the group
List the questions raised by the pairs.

TO READ

One way of answering such questions is to use picture language, or models, rather like working models are used to demonstrate how the real thing might work. The Bible has a number of models or pictures of God, such as King, Sovereign, Judge, Father. The significance of models changes with changing circumstances and sometimes models have to be updated, or new ones found. The model of God as the Shepherd, for example, means little to the modern urban person. One such new model might be God as Artist.

The artist in any field gives being to a work of art. It is he or she who makes it what it is. Admittedly, pre-existent materials are used; but of the work of art as such the artist alone is the creator – it is out of the artist's spontaneity that the work of art comes into being. (page 15)

The artist is reaching out towards a vision or possibility which is not yet fully formulated even in 'the inward eye', and which appears with increasing clarity only as the work proceeds. (page 151)

This model can be refined; God the Sculptor:

Once the medium (a block of stone or wood) is chosen, then it imposes it own constraints. In the artist's mind is a clear idea of the intended shape; but certain unforeseen factors may intervene. The material used may have a grain, a knot or an imperfection which resists the creative intention; or a cut may be made which is actually 'wrong', in the sense of not being exactly what was intended. It is here that the greatness of the artist appears in the skill and patience needed to 'win back' that which is 'wrong'. The wrong is not simply left as it is, nor is it eliminated or cast aside. Still less is the whole work abandoned. The great artist wins back that which is wrong, works with peculiar intensity to find a way by which that imperfection or error may be made to contribute to the total vision rather than detract from it, to enrich it rather than impoverish it. This struggle to win back, and the capacity to do so, is mysterious and difficult to analyse, but anyone who has ever created anything will be well aware of it. It is the exercise of a special and unique kind of 'control' – a control which redeems rather than prevents the wrong, which draws into the overall purpose that which obstructs that purpose. The control of the artist is a 'saving' rather than a 'programming' form of control. 'Creation' is also a continuing 'redemption'. (page 152)

In pairs
Discuss how the model of God the Sculptor might be used to begin to answer the questions listed in the first TO DO.

In fours (two pairs together)
One pair asks the question: How might the model of God the Sculptor be used to begin to answer the questions? The other

pair gives the answers it has been discussing. After five minutes, reverse the roles for a further five minutes.

Discuss the experience, and the strengths and weaknesses of the model.

In the group
Share the findings of the fours.

TO READ

One of the weaknesses of the artist model is that it does not take into account the existence in creation of human beings with wills of their own. If a statue were to come alive, its relationship with the sculptor would be totally changed. A further model is needed.

This is the model of parent and child. The parents are (in a sense) the 'creator' of their child; but the child is endowed with its own independence, its own free will, and the relationship of the parents to the child may become the arena for a prolonged tussle of wills. Parents consider they know what is best for the child: the child believes it knows better. In the early stages the parents may have to use force or material sanctions to impose their will on the child. But as the child grows into adulthood it becomes physically independent of them. They experience the joy and the risk of letting the child be itself. (page 154)

The relationship is one of love. The children may turn away from the right path, but in the Old Testament the Father is ever faithful and long-suffering, giving them another chance. In the New Testament, the Father gives his children new resources and new opportunities to fulfil his will. And

If the children continue to disobey their father, to spurn his gifts and promises, and to prefer their own independence, is the father not hurt? If the model of father and children allows us to talk of the father's love, surely we can press the analogy and say that the father suffers from the disobedience of his children, that the creator, by loving his creation, makes himself vulnerable to being spurned and abused by them? (page 156)

The idea that God loves his creatures as a father loves his children and consequently suffers when his creatures fail to respond to that love enables believers to confront the problem of evil with renewed confidence. God is not aloof from his creatures; he suffers when they suffer. And the fact of his suffering has enabled many to bear and accept their own suffering.

PRAY

Spend five minutes in the group in silence.

Write down one thing that you want to say about God or to God as Creator.

Say aloud these sentences in turn slowly, with pauses between them.

Sing or say together this verse of 'When I survey the wondrous Cross':

Were the whole realm of nature mine,
That were an offering far too small,
Love so amazing, so divine,
Demands my soul, my life, my all.

End by saying the grace together.

PONDER

New life is given, but always has to be given through dying. This is the significance of Christian baptism. We are baptised, according to St Paul, into the death of Jesus and into his burial, in order that we may enter into his resurrection life and become, together, his Body, alive in this world with a life which is already 'hidden with Christ in God', and will there endure eternally.

It is, therefore, precisely because they are Christ's Body in this world, baptised into the pattern of his death and resurrection, that Christians are those who enter into the long-suffering patience of God, sharing his victory over evil by absorbing it in inexhaustible forgiveness, and waiting with him in sure and certain hope of the ultimate triumph of love. The nature of this triumph is revealed unmistakably in the Gospel stories of the first Easter Day. Jesus returns to his friends in a new and transcendent life and power; but the love and forgiveness that marked his earthly existence are unchanged, and the Risen Body still bears the scars and wounds of the Crucified. To pick up our earlier analogy, in the hands of the divine artist what went 'wrong' has become the central feature of an even greater work: 'See my hands and my feet, that it is I, myself.'

The Resurrection does not cancel or merely redress the truth that shines from the cross; it confirms it. This is the eternal nature of divine power and victory, insofar as our human minds are capable of grasping it. (page 161)

God will never turn back from the love which binds him to the world and which remains his way with the world to the end of time. It is a way that embraces the 'changes and chances', in all their arbitrary freedom, within the 'eternal changelessness' of a love that bears, believes, hopes, endures all things. By its very nature that love is at once the source of the grace we need in this life, and our hope of glory in the life to come. (page 162)

THE TALETELLERS

The *Taletellers* have worked together for many years with group a parish level, experimenting with different kinds of study mate and creating new ideas to help others grow in the Christian fa

They are:

The Revd Paul Bates	Director of Training, Diocese of Winchester.
The Revd David Conner	Vicar of Great St Mary's Church, Cambridge.
The Rt Revd Bill Ind	Bishop of Grantham. Member of the Doctrine Commission which produced *We Believe in God*.
The Revd Alec Knight	Priest-in-charge of Easton and Martyr Worthy, near Winchester.
The Revd Robert Teare	Vicar of Holy Trinity and St John's, Winchester.
Mrs Janet Tomlinson	Assistant Lecturer, Cricklade College, Andover.

The *Taletellers* have also produced a series of illustrated study guides which will resource and stimulate groups at parish level to grow in their Christian faith and face the exciting challenge of relating it to everyday life.

The *Taletellers* series of Study Guides is not simply an exercise in absorbing information, nor does it offer cosy, safe, comfortable answers to life's questions. It makes connections – sometimes disturbing – between the biblical story and the stories of ordinary human beings trying to be disciples of Christ in the modern world. *Taletellers* starts from where people *are*, with their real anxieties, problems, hopes, fears and joys. To be involved in *Taletellers* is risky and there are no cut and dried answers. But to those groups who want to open themselves to each other and to the profound insights of life with God this course of learning will be a rich and rewarding journey.

The first six titles in the *Taletellers* series are:

Let There Be . . . And There Was
The Story of Creation

Expelled from Eden
The Story of Adam and Eve

Us and Them
The Story of Cain and Abel

A Matter of Life and Death
The Story of Noah

A Tower and a City
The Story of Babel

You Called?
The Story of Abraham